HOT TOPICS

DINOSAURS

zigzag

Useful internet websites

Check these out to find out more about dinosaurs:

http://www.nhm.ac.uk
Take a virtual tour of the dinosaur exhibits at London's Natural History Museum.
Click on the 'Quick Index' to go straight to the dino pages.

http://www.zoomdinosaurs.com
Discover the biggest, oldest and smallest dinosaurs and conquer all of those
dino myths with fascinating fact sheets.

http://www.ucmp.berkeley.edu/fosrec
This site is all about fossils and why they're so important. Includes dino activities too.

http://www.ucmp.berkeley.edu/diapsids
Find out what's myth and what's fact at the University of California's Museum of
Palaeontology. Includes links to more dino sites.

http://www.kidsdomain.com/brain/dino
This site will keep you entertained for hours with dinosaur riddles and jokes,
great Clip Art, games and clever dinocrafts!

http://www.factmonster.com
This is a great source of monster facts, complete with mind-boggling quizzes and
entertaining activities. Click 'Science' on the home page, then go to 'Animals'.

http://www.brainpop.com/science/plantsandanimals/dinosaurs
Learn how to identify bones with Bob the Rat, watch a dino movie and
discover prehistoric facts. You can also take part in lots of fun activities.

http://www.nationalgeographic.com
Do a search for 'dinosaurs' and find loads of articles about recent discoveries, then take
part in an online egg hunt.

http://www.bbc.co.uk/dinosaurs
This site is a must-see! Includes great illustrated fact files and other info from
the makers of the British TV programme, 'Walking with Dinosaurs'.

http://www.acnatsci.org/dinofest/kids/kids.html
Take a tour of the dinosaur exhibition at the Academy of Natural Sciences.

Written by John Cooper
Illustrated by Peter Bull
Designed by Chris Leishman
Cover designed by Clare Sleven

Editor: Rasha Elsaeed
Assistant designer: Gemma Cooper

© 2003 Zigzag Children's Books,
an imprint of Chrysalis Children's Books,
64 Brewery Road, London N7 9NT

British Library Cataloguing in Publication Data
for this book is available from the British Librar

ISBN 1 904516 06 8

Printed and bound in China

Contents

4

What are dinosaurs?

Diplodocus

An unusual early reptile was Longisquama which lived in Asia 240 million years ago. Only 15 cm long, its back carried a row of stiff, tall scales.

Dinosaurs lived millions of years ago. They were reptiles, a group of animals that today includes lizards and snakes, turtles and tortoises, crocodiles and alligators.

Triceratops

Tsintaosaurus

Q How many different types of dinosaur are there?

A Scientists have grouped dinosaurs into several sorts:

 THERAPODS All the meat-eating, two-legged dinosaurs like Tyrannosaurus.

 SAUROPODS The giant plant-eating dinosaurs like Apatosaurus and Diplodocus.

 ORNITHOPODS Smaller, plant-eating dinosaurs which walked on two legs like Iguanodon and the duck-billed dinosaurs or hadrosaurs. such as Tsintaosaurus.

 CERATOPSIANS The horned dinosaurs like Triceratops, all plant-eaters.

 STEGOSAURS The dinosaurs armed with plates like Stegosaurus. They were plant-eaters and walked on four legs.

 ANKYLOSAURS This group includes other armoured dinosaurs like Nodosaurus. Like the stegosaurs, they were plant eaters and four-footed.

 PACHYCEPHALOSAURS The name means 'thick-headed' and describes a group of dinosaurs with very thick skulls, named after the best known, Pachycephalosaurus.

Q When did dinosaurs live ?

A Dinosaurs lived only during the Mesozoic Era or so-called Age of Reptiles. The Mesozoic Era lasted from 228 million to 64 million years ago. No one has ever seen a dinosaur. The earli of human ancestors did not appear on Earth until 4 million years ago.

Q Were dinosaurs the first reptiles?

A Many other types of reptile lived before the dinosaurs. The very earliest reptile that scientists have recognised was found in Scotland in 1989 in rocks 335 million years old.

Tanystropheus was a 3-metre long early reptile which lived 250 million years ago. Its neck was incredibly long.

The sprawl of an early reptile (left) and the upright legs of a dinosaur (right).

Tyrannosaurus

Stegosaurus

Pachycephalosaurus

Nodosaurus

Q Where did the dinosaurs come from?

A Fossil evidence shows that a group of reptiles living in Argentina about 230 million years ago developed a new way of walking.

Instead of walking with sprawling steps like crocodiles, they began to walk with their legs more directly under their bodies, like the dinosaurs. One reptile called *Lagosuchus* may have been the ancestor of all the dinosaurs.

Q How do you tell the difference between dinosaurs and other fossil reptiles?

A Two important things make a dinosaur. First, they all lived on the land. Second, they all walked on upright legs. All other reptiles, whether fossil or living had different ways of moving.

Q Did all the dinosaurs live at the same time?

A The dinosaurs lived throughout the Mesozoic Era. Different sorts lived different times.

Q What was the very first dinosaur?

A What is believed to be the world's oldest dinosaur was found in Argentina in 1991. Named *Eoraptor*, it lived 228 million years ago. It was over one metre long, perhaps the size of a large dog. Other early dinosaurs have been found in South America and even older ones may still be discovered.

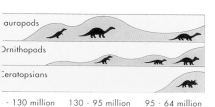

Sauropods

Ornithopods

Ceratopsians

- 130 million years ago | 130 - 95 million years ago | 95 - 64 million years ago

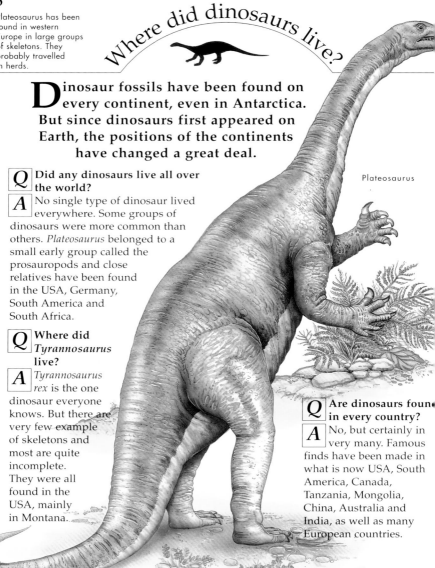

Plateosaurus has been found in western Europe in large groups of skeletons. They probably travelled in herds.

Where did dinosaurs live?

Dinosaur fossils have been found on every continent, even in Antarctica. But since dinosaurs first appeared on Earth, the positions of the continents have changed a great deal.

Q Did any dinosaurs live all over the world?

A No single type of dinosaur lived everywhere. Some groups of dinosaurs were more common than others. *Plateosaurus* belonged to a small early group called the prosauropods and close relatives have been found in the USA, Germany, South America and South Africa.

Q Where did *Tyrannosaurus* live?

A *Tyrannosaurus rex* is the one dinosaur everyone knows. But there are very few example of skeletons and most are quite incomplete. They were all found in the USA, mainly in Montana.

Plateosaurus

Q Are dinosaurs found in every country?

A No, but certainly in very many. Famous finds have been made in what is now USA, South America, Canada, Tanzania, Mongolia, China, Australia and India, as well as many European countries.

continents today are still moving.
th America and Europe are
ng apart from each other about
ast as a fingernail grows.

Pachycephalosaurus and its relatives had
skulls up to 25 cms thick on top! Scientists
have guessed that head-butting contests
were held to defend territory or for rivals
to fight over the leadership of a herd.

Q How could the same dinosaurs live on different continents - did they swim across the ocean?

A For many millions of years, they would not have needed to. The continents have been drifting apart slowly ever since they were formed. Today, *Brachiosaurus* can be found in two continents - Africa and North America. When *Brachiosaurus* was alive it was still all one continent.

Q Did dinosaurs have homes?

A The largest dinosaurs may have had favourite resting places on the edges of forests or beneath cliffs. The smaller dinosaurs could perhaps nestle in more sheltered spots safe from their enemies.

Q Did dinosaurs always live in one place?

A Some herbivorous dinosaurs may have migrated in search of fresh grazing.

) Were dinosaurs in the Antarctic cold?

The Earth's climate was much warmer during the dinosaur's reign. e continent we now call Antarctica s much nearer to the Equator. The osaurs would not have seen any -caps! Reptiles cannot survive y cold climates.

When Gideon Mantell first showed his dinosaur teeth to other scientists of the day, they were identified as being from a rhinoceros!

Early in the nineteenth century, some strange fossils were found in southern England. They were recognised as being from creatures entirely new to science. No-one really knew what these creatures looked like.

Q When were the first dinosaurs found?

A Gideon Mantell, a doctor from Sussex, found the teeth of Iguanodon in 1822. In 1824, William Buckland described some bones which he called Megalosaurus, but found some years before. After these discoveries, many people began to hunt for the fossil bones of these new giant lizards.

Iguanodon got its name because its teeth looked like giant versions of the living marine iguana from the Galapagos.

Q Why didn't anyone ever find them before?

A We know that dinosaur bones were found but no-one realised that they had once belonged to huge extinct reptiles. One bone was thought to be from a giant man!

Q Why do dinosaurs have such funny names?

A Each dinosaur is given a special name using words made up from two ancient languages, Latin and Greek. The names usually mean something which describes the creature in some way. *Megalosaurus* means 'big lizard'. The same dinosaur names are used by scientists of all nationalities.

hundreds of years, the Blackfoot Indians of Canada thought that the dinosaur bones they found were the remains of their ancestors!

Dinosaur teeth have been collected by Chinese doctors for over 2000 years. They are believed to come from dragons and are ground into powder and used for medicines!

Q What did they think dinosaurs looked like when they first found their bones?

A Gideon Mantell drew the first reconstruction of a dinosaur in 1835. He first thought that *Iguanodon* must have been like a giant lizard 21 metres long. We now know that it is about 10 metres long. In 1854, several life-size models of dinosaurs were built in the gardens of Crystal Palace, London. *Iguanodon* is still there to-day, looking rather like a rhinoceros!

Q When was the first complete skeleton of a dinosaur found?

A The first was also one of the most spectacular finds ever. In 1878, almost 40 skeletons of Iguanodon were found in a coal mine in Belgium.

Megalosaurus was the first dinosaur to get a scientific name.

Q Who gave dinosaurs their name?

A Dinosaur means 'terrible lizard'. The name was invented by a famous scientist called Richard Owen in 1842.

Q What was the first dinosaur to be found in North America?

A Huge numbers of dinosaurs have been found in North America. The first was an early sauropod called *Anchisaurus*, found near Manchester, Connecticut, USA. Some fragments were found in 1818 and were thought to be human! By 1855 it was decided that they must be reptilian.

What did dinosaurs look like?

'Supersaurus' had a shoulder blade 2.5 metres long!

When complete skeletons are found, scientists can be fairly sure that they can put the bones together in the right order. But could we guess what you look like just from your skeleton?

Q How do scientists know how to put dinosaur bones together?

A Scientists use their knowledge of other animals to put dinosaur skeletons together. But for a long time after dinosaurs were first discovered, many mistakes were made. Apatosaurus even got the wrong head for nearly 100 years because it was originally found without one!

Early this century, some scientists thought that the legs of Diplodocus sprawled like a lizard. But its chest would have dragged along the ground!

Q Were dinosaurs fat or thin?

A It is difficult to tell if a dinosaur was fat or thin as fossils are usually just the remains of their hard parts - normally bones and teeth. Modern plant-eaters such as elephants, hippos and cattle have big stomachs - and plant-eating dinosaurs were probably just as fat. Smaller, more agile dinosaurs needed to be slimmer to move quickly. Scientists and artists have to use comparisons like this to get an idea of how each dinosaur might havelooked.

Q What was the smallest dinosaur?

A Perhaps the smallest dinosaur was *Compsognathus*. Fully grown it was only 70 cms long and most of this was a long tail.

Compsognathus

Mamenchisaurus was 22
metres long but 10 metres of
was its neck! It lived in China
million years ago.

Gideon Mantell thought that an odd
spike-shaped bone he found must be
a horn on the nose of Iguanodon. It
turned out to be a thumb!

What was dinosaur skin like?

A few fossils of dinosaur skin have
been found. It was tough, dry,

waterproof and
made of small
rounded scales.
Sometimes there
armour plating.

What was the biggest dinosaur?

The largest complete skeleton
known is of *Brachiosaurus* - 12
tres tall, 23 metres long and
ighing 70 tonnes. The longest
osaur known is *Diplodocus*,
ose skeleton was up to 27
tres long. But some new
ds from Colorado and New
xico might be from even
ger dinosaurs. '*Supersaurus*',
trasaurus' and the largest
ismosaurus' were truly
gantic. *Seismosaurus* would have
en similar to *Diplodocus* but may
ve been over 36 metres long and
eighed up to 130 tonnes! This
would have been the
biggest animal ever
to have lived.

Brachiosaurus

lodocus

Q If no-one has seen a dinosaur, how can scientists be sure that they get dinosaurs to look right?

A We can never be sure what
dinosaurs looked like. Scientists
still argue about the way many dinosaurs
might have appeared. Even well-known
dinosaurs like Iguanodon can be made
to look quite different when drawn in
different poses.

Q What colour were dinosaurs?

A Even fossils of skin cannot tell us
what colour it was. Modern
reptiles, especially the lizards, have a
wonderful variety of colours and
patterns and dinosaurs may have been
just as colourful. Bright patches of
colour might have been important for
the dinosaurs to recognise each other
and to display warning signs. The large
plant-eating dinosaurs were
probably camouflaged.
But would we have
guessed at the
zebra's stripes
with only
bones to
study?

What did dinosaurs eat?

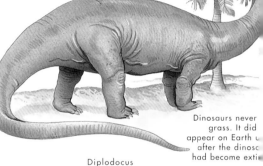

Eucoplocephalus stunned its attackers with the bony club on the end of its tail.

Some dinosaurs had up to 2,000 teeth.

Some dinosaurs ate only plants. Others ate only meat. Plant-eating animals are called herbivores and meat-eating animals are called carnivores.

Q Which dinosaurs ate only plants?

A Most dinosaurs ate plants. The huge sauropods, the largest of all the dinosaurs are the best known. They had long bodies, tails and necks, and small heads with special teeth for grazing. With their long necks they could reach up into trees.

Dinosaurs never grass. It did appear on Earth u after the dinosc had become exti

Diplodocus

Q How can you tell what a dinosaurs ate?

A Fossils of the teeth and jaws are the most important clues. Narrow, curved, sharp teeth belong

to the carnivores like *Tyrannosaurus*. Herbivorous dinosaurs have flatter, grinding teeth like *Camarasaurus*, or sharp nipping teeth like *Iguanodon*. *Ceratopsians* had beaks to help tear off leaves.

Q How did dinosaurs protect themselves from attack?

A Many dinosaurs were protected by armour. This included hard plates, horns and spikes.

Stegosauru

nt-eating dinosaurs
llowed stones to
grind leaves up in
r stomachs.

Fossils of dinosaur droppings have helped scientists discover what dinosaurs ate. But which dropping came from which dinosaur?

Q How did dinosaurs kill?

A Carnivorous dinosaurs had sharp claws as well as sharp teeth: both uld have made good weapons. me large carnivores, like *rannosaurus* may have used their avy skulls as battering rams.

Q Did dinosaurs eat each other?

A Some carnivores were fast and would ve chased other nosaurs, perhaps even ir own kind. They y have hunted in cks like hyaenas. Small *Coelophysis* eletons were found in an adult *elophysis*. Large carnivores, like *rannosaurus*, were too heavy to chase y and perhaps fed off dead or wer moving dinosaurs.

Q How much did dinosaurs eat?

A Plant-eating dinosaurs ate most of the time to get enough nourishment. *Diplodocus* ate about a tonne of ves a day! The meat-eating dinosaurs' t was much richer so they did not need eat huge quantities regularly.

Q What else was there for dinosaurs to eat?

Small reptiles, birds, fish and insects were all food for the dinosaurs.

Tyrannasaurus teeth were more than 15 cm long and very sharp for slicing and tearing at flesh.

No one knows what Tyrannosaurus used its very short arms for as they did not even reach its mouth!

Tyrannosaurus measured 14 metres in length and stood almost 6 metres high.

Could dinosaurs run?

The arrangement of the bones in the ankles and feet of dinosaurs show that all except the sauropods and stegosaurs could run, and footprints prove that they did!

Dryosaurus

Ceratosaurus

Q How fast could dinosaurs run?

A A trackway made by *Tyrannosaurus* shows that it could have outrun a charging rhinoceros, perhaps reaching 30 miles per hour. The fastest of all was a small two-footed dinosaur which left footprints showing that it could run at nearly 45 miles per hour: but we don't know which dinosaur it was! The great sauropod dinosaurs like *Apatosaurus* walked at a speed of only 3 - 5 miles per hour.

Q Did dinosaurs leave any other marks but footprints?

A In only very rare cases, marks have been found where dinosaur tails dragged along the ground. Generally though, despite the enormous size of some tails, they were held up above the ground, and not just when running.

Just as lions hunt zebras today, the meat-eating dinosaurs hunted the plant-eaters. The carnivores ran to catch - the herbivores ran to escape.

Q Could dinosaurs hop, skip, or jump?

A Once, some footprints were believed to have been made by a hopping dinosaur but are now thought to have been made by a turtle swimming in shallow water. Footprints have been found showing a dinosaur with a missing toe, and another with a limp! Scientists believe that at least the active therapods could jump, but there is no evidence from footprints! Ninety-nine out of a hundred trackways show walking dinosaurs.

...sil footprints give us clues about the ...e of the foot as well as the weight ... speed of the dinosaur. There are ...etimes skin impressions too.

Though many dinosaurs could run well, they may not have been able to run for long distances before becoming exhausted.

Q Where are fossil footprints found?

A Throughout the world there are about a thousand places where ...nosaur tracks have been found. One ... the most famous is at the Davenport ...nch in Texas, in rocks 100 million ...ars old. There, and in nearby places, ...ousands of footprints have been found.

Q Are there any footprints of young dinosaurs?

A One of the Texas trackways contains the footprints left by 23 ...uropod dinosaurs which seem to have ...en travelling as a herd. Many of them ...e quite small, probably youngsters. ...e larger members of the herd travelled ... front and at the sides of the herd, the ...aller ones were rotected in the centre.

Q How can footprints be fossilised?

A Dinosaurs crossing muddy lake or sea shores left behind their footprints, just as animals do today. If the mud dries in the hot sun, the next tide or flood washes more mud into the imprints which are then preserved.

Q Which dinosaurs could run the fastest?

A The dinosaurs which could run the fastest had two long hind legs, and were small and slim. *Hypsilophodon* from England and *Lesothosaurus* from southern Africa were both herbivores that could run fast.

Lesothosaurus

Could dinosaurs swim?

Plesiosaurs have long necks, short bodies and large paddle-like limbs, rather like modern sea-lions.

Like any land-living animals today - elephants, hippopotamuses and buffaloes - dinosaurs enjoyed a good paddle and swim.

Q Were any dinosaurs amphibious?

A This was an old idea. It was once thought that the heaviest dinosaurs like *Brachiosaurus* and *Apatosaurus* were too large to support their own weight on land, and therefore had to live in water. Scientists have now calculated that their large leg bones were strong enough to support them out of the water.

Q If the Loch Ness monster really does exist, wouldn't it be a swimming dinosaur?

A If Nessie ever was found and proved to be a reptile, she would almost certainly turn out to be a plesiosaur, ichthyosaur or pliosaur. These were all marine reptiles and were not dinosaurs, which only lived on land.

Q Did any dinosaurs live permanently in the water?

A Probably not but ideas change. The long necks of dinosaurs like *Mamenchisaurus* were once thought to be useful for breathing in deep water. Unfortunately, water pressure at those depths - 10 metres or more - would not have allowed the lungs to work.

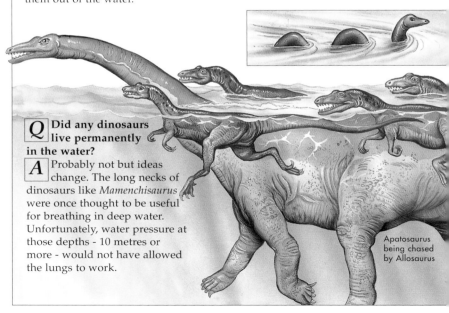

Apatosaurus being chased by Allosaurus

...yosaurs looked ...er like modern ...ks and dolphins.

Many modern creatures like dogs, elephants, polar bears and even cows can swim. They don't need flippers or webbed feet and dinosaurs may have been able to swim just as well.

Did the swimming reptiles live at the same time as the dinosaurs?

Throughout the reign of the dinosaurs, the ichthyosaurs and ...siosaurs were very common in the seas ... oceans of the world. There were ...ny types, including the pliosaurs and ...smosaurs. The largest of all was an ...stralian pliosaur called *Kronosaurus* ...ich grew as large as 13 metres.

Could dinosaurs float?

Despite the enormous size of some, there is no reason to suppose that ... dinosaur would sink. One set of ...ntosaur footprints shows only ...ressions from the front feet! It seems ... the dinosaur was floating in a lake ... simply kicked itself along with its ...nt feet.

Q Could dinosaurs have fed under water?

A Perhaps, for water plants would be good food. Dinosaurs with weak teeth like the ankylosaurs may have grazed rather like hippos or like ducks in shallow water.

The long hollow crest of *Parasaurolophus* was once thought to be a sort of snorkel used while feeding below the water.

Q Did any dinosaurs have flippers to help them swim?

A There may be one dinosaur that did. One species of *Compsognathus* found in Germany seems to have had flipper-like front legs. No-one is sure, but perhaps they allowed it to swim extra quickly to catch prey or escape from its own hunters.

Could dinosaurs fly?

Longisquama glided through the air with its long scaly wings.

Some small dinosaurs have skeletons almost identical to *Archaeopteryx* - the oldest known bird. The dinosaur ancestors of the birds must have developed the ability to fly or glide short distances.

Q How well could *Archaeopteryx* fly?

A Probably not very well. Compared to modern birds its muscles were weak and it was much heavier. But it could have flapped its wings quite well and its bony, feathered tail would have made a good rudder to help it manoeuvre on long glides through the air.

Q How did dinosaurs get feathers?

A Reptile scales like those on snakes and lizards may have become 'feathery' to help keep the smaller dinosaurs warm. Only later did they also prove useful for flying.

Q How did the dinosaurs learn to fly?

A Perhaps like many living animals (including frogs, squirrels an monkeys), small, feathered dinosaurs began to jump, glide and parachute from tree to tree, chasing prey or escaping from danger.

chaeopteryx was discovered in
rmany in rocks 150 million years
. Alongside its fossil bones are
ar impressions of feathers
ming two wings and a tail.

The Dodo lived on the island of
Mauritius in the Indian Ocean.
Because it could not fly it was easily
hunted and became extinct by the
end of the sixteenth century.

Q How could giants like dinosaurs have flown?

A *Tyrannosaurus* would never have got airborne! Some carnivorous dinosaurs though, like Compsognathus and Ornitholestes, were very small, lightly built with hollow bones and could run quickly. Perhaps they chased small lizards and insects and began to take to the air.

Q Are there any other fossil birds?

A Fossils of birds are very rare: their light hollow bones do not fossilise well. Examples that have been found include birds similar to large terns, ostriches, eagles and the Dodo.

Q Isn't a Pteranodon a flying dinosaur?

A No. Although they lived on Earth at the same time as the dinosaurs, *Pteranodons* belong to a group of flying reptiles, called pterosaurs.

Pteranodon

Q How did pterosaurs learn to fly before the dinosaurs?

A The skeletons of the earliest known flying reptiles are similar to ancient carnivorous reptiles alive before the dinosaurs. Their skeletons were light and perhaps they too, like the later feathered dinosaurs climbed trees and learnt to glide.

When dinosaur eggs are found, it is not always possible to say which dinosaur laid them.

Did dinosaurs have babies?

All living creatures reproduce and dinosaurs were no exception. It is believed that, like almost all living reptiles, dinosaurs laid eggs.

Q Have any fossil dinosaur eggs ever been found?

A Yes. The first ones found were discovered in the Gobi desert of Mongolia in 1921. They were neatly arranged in nests and were discovered with skeletons of the small horned dinosaur, *Protoceratops*.

Q Did all dinosaurs lay eggs?

A Fossil eggs have been found with sauropods, ceratopsians and a variety of other dinosaurs. However, they are very rare and the majority of dinosaurs have left no fossil eggs. But most scientists assume that all dinosaurs did lay eggs.

Q What do dinosaur eggs look like?

A Unlike most modern reptiles, dinosaurs seem to have laid eggs with hard shells. Eggs that have been found whole are usually oval - shaped, blunt at one end with a wrinkled surface. In the case of *Protoceratops*, they were about 20 cms long and laid in nests up to 30 or more at a time. Other eggs are usually between 120 and 170 mm long (as big as an ostrich egg).

A mother Maiasaura with her babies.

s of the dinosaurs
dromeus and Troodon
e been x-rayed and
ain the tiny fossilised
es of embryos.

Some fossils of Chasmosaurus
show that in herds, they
formed a protective circle
around their young to guard
them from attack.

A herd of
Chasmosaurus

Were dinosaurs good parents?

Even the fiercest alligator living
today is a very caring parent,
ding and protecting its tiny young.
e remains of *Maiasaura* dinochicks
re found in Montana. Though their
th show wear from eating, they were
l in their nests. They must have been
by their parents until they grew old
ugh to leave home.

**How did young dinosaurs tell
their mothers from their fathers?**

Scientists can only guess whether a
fossilised dinosaur is male or
male. In a few examples where many
letons have been found together,
ne are bigger than others - perhaps
males. We can be sure that baby
osaurs knew the difference

Q **Are there any fossils of baby
dinosaurs?**

A The smallest dinosaur skeleton is
only 20 cms long - about the size of
a blackbird. It has been called
Mussaurus (mouse-lizard) but it is in fact
a very young dinochick of a yet-
unknown dinosaur. Other dinosaur
babies found include *Protoceratops*,
Maiasaura, *Psittacosaurus*
and *Coelophysis*.

Baby
Maiasaura

Q **Did the gigantic sauropods lay
gigantic eggs?**

A The largest eggs found weighed
7 kgs in weight - not much
compared to 20 tonne sauropods!

Is this what *Stenonychosaurus* might have looked like if it had continued evolving?

Were dinosaurs stupid?

The original discoverers of *Apatosaurus* and *Diplodocus* were surprised at the small size of the heads compared to the bodies of the dinosaurs. They thought that with such tiny brains, the dinosaurs must have had little intelligence. Today, we are not so sure.

Q Which was the cleverest dinosaur?

A Size for size, *Stenonychosaurus* must have been the brightest dinosaur. Its brain is similar in proportion to birds and even some mammals, and much bigger than crocodiles.

Q Does a large brain mean that a dinosaur was clever?

A Brains control behaviour and the senses, as well as cleverness. The small carnivorous dinosaurs had large brains compared to the size of their bodies. As a result they had excellent vision, could move quickly and were good at learning how to hunt and catch their prey.

Stenonychosaurus

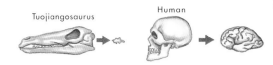

brain of the Chinese
osaur Tuojiangosaurus
ghed only 70 - 80 grams.

Tuojiangosaurus

Human

How big were dinosaur brains?

For reptiles, most dinosaurs seem to have had quite large brains. The aller, faster carnivores had the largest ins, though the largest of all was haps *Tyrannosaurus*. The stegosaurs 1 perhaps the smallest brains - about size of a walnut!

Q How do you measure the brain of a dinosaur?

A Sometimes, when mud and sand surrounded a dinosaur skull after death, it filled the brain cavity too. The result - a fossil brain! Different areas of the brain can be seen as well as the bony passages for nerves and blood vessels.

Which dinosaurs were the most stupid?

The sauropods score lowest in the brain stakes. But however small their brains were, they were obviously good enough for them to survive as a group for 150 million years.

Q Did the enormous sauropods have enormous brains?

A Not necessarily so. Brains do not automatically get bigger in proportion to bodies. It depends what dinosaurs did. The more active the dinosaur, the larger the brain needed to be to produce quicker reactions.

Do living reptiles have large brains?

On average, crocodile and alligator brains are approximately the same e as similar sized dinosaurs. The brains of living mammals are ten times the size of similar sized living reptiles.

Crocodile

24

Some scientists believe that sauropod dinosaurs like Barosaurus might have had up to 8 hearts to help pump blood up their long necks.

How did their bodies work?

The flesh and organs of all creatures rot away after death. To understand how the bodies of dinosaurs worked, scientists have to build up their ideas on very little evidence.

Q What did dinosaur blood look like?

A Like modern animals, dinosaurs needed blood to carry oxygen, heat and food around their bodies. Their blood was probably much the same as our own. To pump this blood, the dinosaurs needed hearts. Those of the biggest dinosaurs must have been enormous to pump blood to heads as high as 25 metres above the ground.

Q What was a dinosaur's normal body temperature?

A We will never know for sure. Reptiles today keep their bodies warm by sun bathing. This can limit their movement in cold weather, so most reptiles live in warm climates. Mammals and birds rely on their own bodies to release heat from food. If they were as active as we think they were, dinosaurs may have been able to do the same thing. Once the biggest dinosaurs were warm, they would probably never have cooled down!

Q Does fossil bone have fossil blood in it?

A Blood unfortunately does not fossilise, but some bony passages for blood vessels do. Microscopic studies of dinosaur bone have shown that it resembles the bone of living warm-blooded mammals, rather than the so-called cold-blooded living reptiles. This means that the dinosaurs may have been much more active than their living relatives.

Barosaurus

Q How do we know what muscles dinosaurs had?

A Muscles are attached to bones. Because of this, bones carry scars of where the muscles were once fixed. The size and position of these marks on dinosaur bones allow scientists to reconstruct the shapes of legs, arms, hips and shoulders. Living reptiles also give some good clues.

inosaurus had long spines running
n its backbone. These would have been
red with skin to form a 'sail'. It could
m up and cool down by directing its sail
rds or away from the sun.

Gallimimus had very large
eyes. Each eye was
supported in its socket by
a ring of bony plates
which are often fossilised

ranosaurus

Q How big were dinosaur ears?

A There is no evidence that any
dinosaur had outer ears like
elephants or even ourselves. Like
modern reptiles and birds,
dinosaur ears would probably
have been visible on the
surface of their heads. They
would look like circular
marks in the skin.

The nostrils of the duck-bill
dinosaur called
Saurolophus are thought to
have been covered by an
table pouch of skin. Perhaps like many birds,
olophus could blow this up into a large, colourful
on to warn off rivals or to signal to the opposite sex.

How did dinosaurs smell?

Dinosaurs had holes in their skulls
for the nostrils to allow for
athing. They probably used them for
elling too. Some dinosaurs like
arasaurus had very large nostrils on
of the head. Scientists once thought
these helped the dinosaurs to
athe underwater.

Q What colour were dinosaurs' eyes?

A We will never
know the
answer, but the eyes
of living reptiles are usually bright and
yellow. They are not surrounded by
white like our own. Scientists can tell
from dinosaur
skulls that most
had large eyes
and so could
probably see
very well.

Some scientists believe that less than 10 per cent of dinosaur types that ever existed have been found fossilised.

How do you find a dinosaur?

Fossils are found in rocks formed from mud and sand left by water or wind. They are called sedimentary rocks. Identifying the right rocks of the right age is a good start to finding dinosaurs.

Q How do dinosaurs turn into fossils?

A

Dead dinosaur washed into river.

Skeleton buried in mud and sand.

Mud and sand turn into rock, bones into fossils.

Millions of years later erosion reveals the fossils.

Q How do they know if the rocks are old enough to contain dinosaur fossils?

A All sorts of plants and animals lived with the dinosaurs and their fossils are much more common: ferns, snails, freshwater fish, shellfish and even insects. Recognising the right type of rocks with the right type of fossils shows that dinosaurs might be around.

Q How do scientists know where to look for a dinosaur?

A The most common fossils are found in rocks formed under water, especially the seas or oceans. Dinosaurs only lived on the land and so are not so common. They are found in rocks that formed near rivers, lakes, seashores and also deserts.

Q Where do you start to dig?

A Fossils are usually found where the rocks can be seen - quarries, cliffs, or mountains. Fossil hunters then hunt for odd bones sticking out of the rock, made visible by wind and rain. *Baryonyx* was discovered by a man who found only a single claw in a busy quarry. Most of the skeleton was found later by expert excavation.

e of the dinosaur fossils found
this century have still not
fully extracted from the rock
hich they were collected.

Before dinosaur bones are removed
from an excavation they are
coccooned in plaster of paris or foam
jackets to protect them on the journey
back to the laboratory.

Q How do you dig up a dinosaur?

A Excavating a dinosaur is not an easy
job! After discovery, several tons of
k might need to be moved by diggers,
ldozers and pneumatic drills.
mmers and chisels might
used for more careful
rk before a bone
be removed.

Q What do you do with a dinosaur
once it has been dug up?

A Bones may be cracked and only
partly visible in their enclosing
rock. They are taken to laboratories
where the rock is carefully removed
with special tools and cracks are
constantly repaired. It may be years
before all the bones are prepared.
Only if the bones are in very good
condition might they be joined to
make a skeleton.

Q Are there any dinosaurs
left to find?

A Though it is very rare to
find a completely new
dinosaur, *Baryonyx* is a dinosaur unlike
any other, and it was found in 1982. In
Canada, millions of dinosaur bones can
be seen scattered in Dinosaur Provincial
Park: three or four complete skeletons
are found each year.

Dinosaur skeletons in museums are often plaster casts
moulded from the real bones. Dinosaurs are too
precious to risk damage .

Diplodocus
skeleton

Because dinosaur skeletons are rarely complete, model
bones are often added to the real skeleton to make up
for any that are missing.

How do you become an expert?

You can collect dinosaur models, toys, games and even postage stamps from around the world.

The study of fossils is called palaeontology 'old-life study'). Many years of learning are needed to become a palaeontologist, but there are lots of ways to become interested in dinosaurs.

Make a catalogu an exercise book help you remem' what the fossils and what you kr about them.

Q **What do you have to study at school to become a dinosaur expert?**

A All fossils are the remains of once living creatures so biology is important. Mathematics and English will always be useful and later, physics and chemistry.

Q **Can you learn about dinosaurs a university?**

A There are no courses especially about dinosaurs. At university you learn about different aspects of geology - rocks, minerals and fossils, and the processes that have made and shaped the Earth. You could also study zoology and learn about living animals before specialising in dinosaur studies.

Q **How can I find dinosaur fossils?**

A It helps if you live in an area wher dinosaur fossils are known to occu but you would still have to be very lucky. The commonest dinosaur finds a probably teeth. Start by making a collection of other fossils to get experience. Leaflets and books may be found in libraries, shops and museums.

first dinosaur skeleton to be put together was an Iguanodon
Belgium. It was assembled in 1882. The bones were hung
scaffolding by ropes so that they could be moved until they
ed right. Then they were supported by an iron frame.

Q What do I need to look for fossils?

A A hammer and chisel are useful to split open rocks. Protective clothing is needed too - gloves for hammering, goggles to guard your eyes and a hard hat to protect your head, especially near cliffs.

el-makers and artists must work closely with
eontologists if their models and pictures are to
right. Muscles are carefully drawn onto a
eton outline and the skin added so that the
c shape is right.

Q What do I do if I find a fossil?

A Remove the fossil carefully and wrap it in kitchen roll or toilet tissue. Make a note of where and when you found it. At home, clean away loose dirt with a dry brush. If this does not work, try brushing with a little water. When the fossil is dry write a number on it for use in a catalogue of your finds. Store your fossil safely by making a tissue 'nest' for it in a box or drawer.

Triceratops

Q What tips are there for collecting fossils?

Never collect without the permission of the landowner.

ver collect from cliffs or quarry walls.
s much safer to work on fallen blocks
waste tips.

not be greedy - leave some fossils for
ers to find.

place your poorer fossils when you
d better examples.

Q Can I get any help?

A Visit your local museum and ask if there is a geologist on the staff. If you have collected fossils. someone may help you to identify them. You may also be able to find out if there is a local geological society. Society members will include many enthusiastic collectors. Find out from them about the latest information on dinosaurs.

A popular theory for the death of the dinosaurs is that a 6 mile-wide meteorite, travelling at 60,000 mph hit the Earth.

What happened to dinosaurs?

There are no dinosaurs alive today. One of the great mysteries in the history of life on Earth is why such a successful group of animals should become extinct.

Q When did the dinosaurs become extinct?

A Rocks about 70 million years old, from all over the world contain dinosaur fossils. Amazingly, only 5 or 6 million years later, not a single dinosaur had survived.

Q What was the last type of dinosaur to live?

A It is not always easy to tell whether rocks in one place on Earth are a little bit younger or older than rocks in other places. So, we are not sure if some dinosaurs outlived others thousands of miles away. Certainly the last dinosaur groups included *Tyrannosaurus and Triceratops*. A bone-head dinosaur (pachycephalosaur) called *Stygimoloch* from Montana, USA may have been the very last to survive - but only a few pieces of broken skull have been found.

Q What could have caused the dinosaurs to die out?

A Possible explanations for dinosaur extinction:

Funny	Mistakes	Serious
Boredom - after 150 million years.	Constipation from the new flowering plants.	Competition the mammal
Only male or female dinosaurs left.	Eggs eaten by the mammals.	Climate gett colder.
Too much smoking.	Disease from a new virus.	Brains got smaller.
New caterpillars ate all the leaves.	Holes in the ozone layer caused by radiation.	High temperature caused by a meteorite ex

Q What else became extinct with the dinosaurs?

A All the large marine reptiles - the mosasaurs and plesiosaurs, as well as the flying reptiles, disappeared. Also some types of shellfish, including the ammonites and belemnites, and huge numbers of microscopic marine plants vanished.

Ammonite

Belemnites

...m, a common ...ent in meteorites, ...een found ...dwide in rocks of ...ame age.

In Mexico, fossil tree trunks have been found mixed up with rocks from the ocean floor. These are evidence of the huge tidal waves that a large meteorite would cause.

Q What survived the great extinction?

A The majority of plants and animals survived. These included the other ...tiles such as snakes, lizards, ...codiles and turtles. Birds and the ...y mammals survived too, together ...h shellfish, corals, starfish, insects and ...d plants.

Map of Mexico showing likely area of meteorite impact.

Q What do scientists think is the real reason dinosaurs died out?

A Most scientists now agree that two things caused the death of the dinosaurs and many other creatures. First the climate had been gradually cooling down. Second, around 64 million

Mexico

years ago something catastrophic happened. Some people believe a huge meteriorite struck the Earth.

Q How could a meteorite do so much damage?

A A large meteorite hitting the Earth would throw up a gigantic cloud of dust. This would cut out sunlight for months, perhaps years causing plants and animals to die. Some, like the dinosaurs never recovered.

Q Is it possible that dinosaurs are alive somewhere on Earth?

A Sadly, though there are occasional stories and legends, no one seriously believes that even a small dinosaur could have remained undetected. But dinosaur descendents are still all around us: the birds.

Index